D1711707

ANOREXIA &
BULIMIA

BY
Dayna Wolhart

EDITED BY
Maythee Kantar

CRESTWOOD HOUSE

New York

CIP
LIBRARY OF CONGRESS CATALOGING IN PUBLICATION DATA

Wolhart, Dayna.
Anorexia and bulimia

(Facts about)
Includes index.
SUMMARY: Defines anorexia and bulimia and explains the causes, side-effects, and treatment of these eating disorders.
1. Anorexia nervosa—Juvenile literature. 2. Bulimia—Juvenile literature. [1. Anorexia nervosa. 2. Bulimia.] I. Kantar, Maythee. II. Title. III. Series.
RC552.A5W64   1988   616.85'2—dc19   88-21553
ISBN 0-89686-416-2

International Standard Book Number:	Library of Congress Catalog Card Number:
0-89686-416-2	88-21553

PHOTO CREDITS

Cover: Journalism Services: Scott Wanner
DRK Photo: (Don & Pat Valenti) 37
Third Coast Stock Source: (Howard Linton)18; (Kent Dufault) 7, 27, 41, 42; (Jack Hamilton) 9, 22, 33; (Bob Smith) 10; (William Stonecipher) 14; (William Meyer) 4; (J. P. Slater) 28, 34; (Ralf-finn Hestoft) 30-31
Taurus Photos: (Tim McCabe) 12; (Pam Hasegawa) 13, 16
Viewfinders: (Chris Grajczyk) 20; (Bill McCarthy) 39

53054   91-18024

CRESTWOOD HOUSE

Macmillan Publishing Company
866 Third Avenue
New York, NY 10022
Collier Macmillan Canada, Inc.

Printed in the United States of America
10 9 8 7 6 5 4

TABLE OF CONTENTS

AFRAID OF FOOD

Jennifer is a teenage girl who used to look a lot like most of her friends. But now she is very thin. She has lost so much weight that her thighs are thinner than her knees. Her clothes hang loosely on her. Her skin is wrinkled with patches of dryness. Her hair has begun to fall out in handfuls. Jennifer is starving, but it's not because her family does not have enough to eat. Jennifer has *anorexia nervosa*, an eating problem or "disorder." As thin as she is, Jennifer still thinks she is fat! She eats only tiny bits of food and exercises too much. What has happened to Jennifer?

Sarah is neither fat nor thin, but her weight goes up and down often. Most of Sarah's friends would say she is pretty much like them. In fact, her friends wonder how Sarah can always be so "perfect." She exercises regularly. She talks about how she is always on a diet and the foods she can't eat. Her hair, makeup, and clothes always seem to be just right. Sarah's friends don't know that she is really very troubled. Like Jennifer, Sarah is terrified of being fat. But instead of starving herself all the time, Sarah sometimes eats huge amounts of food. Then she forces herself to vomit or take *laxatives* (drugs that make you have a bowel movement). Sarah has *bulimia,* another eating disorder.

Jennifer and Sarah are in trouble. Both are terribly

It's important to take good care of yourself—and to feel good about yourself.

afraid of being fat. Their daily lives have been taken over by their problems with eating properly. How did they get this way? How many other people are like them? Can they get well?

WHAT IS ANOREXIA?

Anorexia is a severe weight loss and begins when the victim goes on a diet. Anorectics, as people who have anorexia are called, do not have a true picture of how their bodies look. Even after losing as much as one-fourth of their body weight, anorectics say they feel fat.

Anorectics are usually very interested in food. Sometimes they fix fancy meals for their families, but they will not join the family in eating the meal. Anorectics are afraid to eat. They fear that even one bite of the wrong kind of food will make them fat. To burn up as many calories as possible, anorectics usually follow strict exercise programs.

WHAT IS BULIMIA?

Bulimia is a two-part pattern of *binge* eating and *purging* that happens over and over again. During a binge, the bulimic will eat large quantities of food that are very rich and high in sugars and fats. Binges almost always happen in secret. The victim knows that the behavior is not normal, and she feels guilty. She is afraid of not being able to stop.

The second part of bulimia is purging, which may take the form of vomiting, using overdoses of laxatives and *diuretics* (drugs that remove water from the body), or *fasting*. A fast means that a person will go without eating for several days, or will eat very little for several weeks. Thus the bulimic's weight may often change dramatically.

When girls and boys first reach adulthood, they often feel many doubts about themselves.

7

WHO GETS EATING DISORDERS?

Nine out of ten people who get anorexia or bulimia are female. (Because most victims are female, in this book we will refer to an anorectic as "she." However, this does not mean that men and boys never get eating disorders.) The disorders usually develop during the teenage years, though younger and older people may also suffer from them. About one in every 200 to 250 American girls between 12 and 18 will get anorexia, and the numbers are increasing. In the 1950s, about one in 25,000 became anorexic. By the mid 1970s, it was one in 6,000. About one of every ten anorectics will die of the disease. Some recover from the outward signs of anorexia, but commit suicide later in life because they were not able to solve their emotional problems.

Because the symptoms of bulimia are harder to detect, it is much harder to estimate the number of its victims. There may be as many as one million bulimics in the United States. Bulimia is more common than anorexia. It is not as likely to cause death as quickly as the starvation of anorexia.

Anorexia and bulimia can be cured. It is important, however, that people who have these disorders get help as soon as possible. The sooner they are treated, the better their chance for recovery.

Nine out of ten people who get anorexia or bulimia are female.

PERSONAL CHARACTERISTICS

Both anorectics and bulimics set very high goals for themselves. They feel they are failures if they are anything less than perfect. Families and friends are often confused when a loved one develops an eating disorder. Anorectics and bulimics are usually very good students who seem to have few problems. Yet, these seemingly "perfect" young people often have a very low opinion of themselves. They want to please others. They depend on other people to make them feel good about themselves.

If treatment is successful, an anorectic will relearn more normal eating patterns.

Many anorectics and bulimics come from families that are strict and demanding. In these families it is not comfortable to talk about feelings and fears. Family members are not allowed to show their anger or unhappiness, even though everyone feels those emotions sometimes. The anorectic or bulimic may come to feel that she can never live up to her parents' expectations. She feels unable to express her feelings of failure. She may begin to focus on her body. She

10

may seek to control herself through diet and exercise, because she feels unable to control any other areas of her life.

FOOD: HOW MUCH IS ENOUGH?

Food contains *calories*. A calorie is a unit for measuring the amount of energy available in each kind of food. Our bodies change the food we eat into energy. Everything we do requires energy — working, playing, even rest. Our hearts pump; our lungs breathe. A person who does not eat enough or one who eats poorly does not get enough energy to function well.

The average teenage or adult woman needs to eat between 1,800 and 2,500 calories each day to stay healthy. Anorectics have been known to reduce their total daily calories to as little as 300 to 500 calories. Bulimics may take in enough calories overall, but vomiting or taking laxatives can rob the body of vitamins and minerals. This can lead to other kinds of diseases.

The amount of food we need each day is determined by our health and by how active we are. Without thinking about it, most healthy people just naturally eat enough to balance the energy they use.

By eating a variety of nutritious foods and exercising moderately, our bodies tend to stay at about the same "natural" weight. Some nutrition experts refer to this natural weight as our *set-point*. The set-point is different for everyone. The body weight that is right for one person may be too heavy or too light for another.

Studies have shown that the average teenage or adult woman needs to eat 1,800 to 2,500 calories each day.

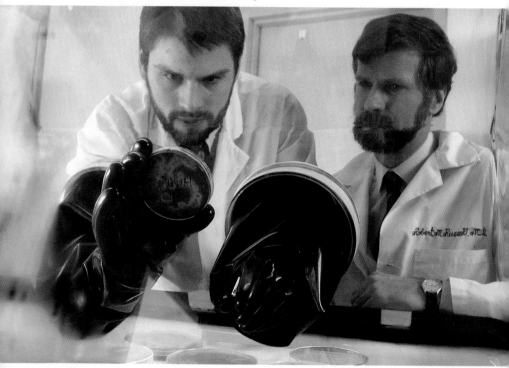

Every person has a different natural weight or "set point."

WHY DO WE WANT TO BE THIN?

Not everyone is happy with his or her natural weight. Many people have the idea that they must be slim to be pretty. Fashion magazines show ultra-slim models. Being thin is equated with being strong and

in control. Fat is considered ugly, a sign of greed, laziness, or lack of self-control. Because of these ideas, about 80% of all women diet. In a recent study, researchers found that almost half of the nine-year-old girls, and eight out of ten of the 10- and 11-year-olds said they were dieting to lose weight. Nearly nine out of ten 17-year-old girls said they were on diets. Of all these girls, fewer than one in five was actually overweight.

If you plan to go on a diet, see a doctor first. The doctor can help you decide how much weight, if any, you need to lose. If the doctor says you are not overweight, talk to him or her about why you want to diet. If you need to lose weight, the doctor can guide you in healthy food choices.

Being thin has not always been as stylish as it is now. In the first ten years of the 1900s, plump women were considered prettier. In the 1920s, a more slender look came into style. By the 1940s and 1950s, the ideal had changed to a rounder shape again. Since the 1970s, a very thin shape has been in style.

Unfortunately, as thinness has become more and more desirable, women have become less active. Many of today's working women sit at a desk in an office. They burn far fewer calories than women 100 years ago. Without as many machines to help do their work, women used to do more hard physical labor. Since we don't burn up as many calories, we must eat

Fashion magazines make people think that only thin people can be pretty.

15

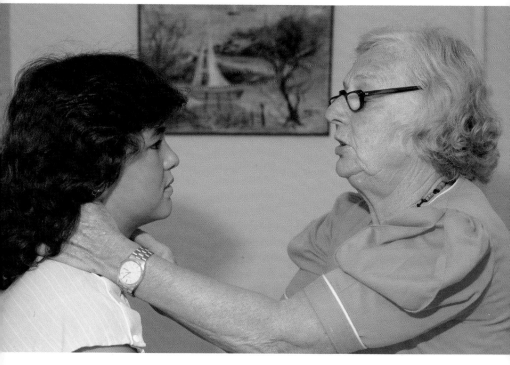

Before dieting, see a doctor who can tell you how much weight you need to lose.

less in order to have a fashionably thin body. As a result, hundreds of books and articles have been written about new ways to lose weight.

Some popular diets offer good nutrition during weight loss. Many of them do not, however. *"Crash" diets* focus on losing a lot of weight in a short time. In order to achieve these weight loss "results," the foods recommended on crash diets are usually very limited. Some diets only allow eating one kind of

16

food, such as fruit. Others forbid eating an entire group of foods, such as breads and cereals. Because these food plans do not allow variety, they can be very dangerous to your health.

WHAT IS SELF-ESTEEM?

Self-esteem is the feeling that we are ok as people — that we are likable for who we are. It's a feeling that we are strong enough to tackle our problems — and win. When we are secure, we feel sure that our parents and friends will still love and care for us even if we make mistakes.

Anorectics and bulimics have low self-esteem. They believe that their looks — instead of their personalities — are the only thing about themselves that others can like. But they are unhappy with their looks. They think their bodies are the main source of all their problems. Many think, "If I were thin, everyone would like me." Or they may think, "As soon as I get to my ideal weight, Mom and Dad will approve of me." Or they may feel, "Fat is disgusting, so I must be disgusting, too."

There are certain times in our lives when our self-esteem is more fragile. At *puberty,* when our bodies

begin to grow to adulthood, we often feel many doubts about ourselves. *Adolescence* is a time when it is common to feel unsure and insecure. It is also a time when we worry more about what our peers think of us. The age of 18-19 is another time of risk. At this age, many people graduate from high school and leave home for the first time. Whether they go to college or to their first full-time job, this is a very threatening time. It is no surprise, then, that many anorectics and bulimics first develop their eating disorders at puberty or in their late teens.

It's important to remember that most people feel bad about themselves at one time or another. Feeling "low" every once in a while is normal. But there are many things you can do to feel better about yourself. Talk about your feelings to your parents, friends, or a trusted adult. Take good care of your health. Learn to see the good in yourself.

FOOD, FEELINGS, AND FAMILIES

For most people, food and eating are much more than the way in which we give our bodies energy. Family mealtimes are a time for talking and sharing. Holidays are a time when many families gather

Self-esteem is a feeling that you can tackle problems and find solutions.

together to celebrate. This usually involves a large or special meal, such as at Thanksgiving. Food and family relations are closely related. Little babies experience their first close human contact when they eat. Their parents hold them, speak softly to them, comfort them. Most people never lose this early sense of food as a source of comfort and a way of showing love.

The relationship of food to feelings and families

Many family holidays and celebrations include eating a big meal.

plays a role in the development of anorexia and bulimia. Many anorectics and bulimics are "good" kids who get good grades, obey their parents, don't get into trouble, and don't seem to have problems. But the problems may be hidden. Anorectics may reject food to show anger and rebellion against the family. Bulimics may turn to food as a source of comfort in an unloving family. They may use binge eating as an escape from the pressures of trying to be perfect.

WHAT HAPPENS TO THE ANORECTIC?

The causes of anorexia are many. They include low self-esteem, an overpowering family, fear of growing up, and the need to be perfect. Many anorectics also have a history of *depression* in their families. Depression is a feeling of hopelessness and unhappiness that lasts a long time. It can make a person more likely to get an eating disorder. Some people develop eating disorders because of a painful event, such as their parents' divorce or the death of a classmate.

Having problems like these does not mean that a person will become anorectic or bulimic, however. Anybody who is feeling depressed, confused, afraid or

When controlled and not excessive, diet and exercise are good ways to keep healthy.

out of control needs to ask for help. A counselor or other trained professional can help people get over their bad feelings.

Both anorexia and bulimia begin with a strict or "crash" diet. At first families and friends find it hard to disapprove. After all, diet and exercise are thought to be healthy. As a person begins to lose weight, she may get compliments. As her weight continues to drop, an anorectic will diet even more harshly and exercise even harder. But she will think she is disgustingly "fat." When others start to worry, the anorectic will not believe them. She may think everyone is jealous and is trying to keep her "fat."

Anorectics say they "like to feel hungry." Hunger pangs assure them that their stomachs are empty, that they are not gaining weight. Even so, they still fear fat and will make themselves exercise to the point of exhaustion—even collapse.

People who overexercise in sports such as gymnastics, swimming, wrestling, or dance may become anorectic or bulimic. They think losing weight will improve their performance.

SYMPTOMS OF ANOREXIA

Anorexia is defined as a loss of 25% or more of normal body weight (for example, a person who should weigh 100 pounds would drop below 75 pounds). Because of their lack of body fat, anorectics often feel chilled. The body may make up for the lack of warmth by producing a fine hair called *lanugo*.

Constipation is common because the person eats too little for the intestines and bowel to work properly. If the girl has begun menstruation, her periods will become irregular or stop. Most anorectics have very dry skin. Their hair may fall out because of poor nutrition. If enough weight is lost, the anorectic will become confused and unable to think clearly. Her brain will not function well because of a lack of protein. Anorexia also disturbs sleep patterns.

In the most severe cases, the anorectic will starve to death. However, if the disease is diagnosed and treated early enough, and if normal eating patterns are regained, anorexia can be cured. Most of the problems are reversible. But the longer the disorder goes untreated, the greater the chance of permanent physical damage.

ONE ANORECTIC'S STORY

Carol is an only child. She was 16 when she developed anorexia. Her father is a successful sales executive and her mother is an alcoholic. Carol recalls, "No matter what I did, it was never good enough for my parents." Carol's mother insisted that she keep her room spotless all the time. When she was drinking, Carol's mother would often find fault and demand that Carol clean her room over and over.

Carol did well in school, even though she was quiet and shy. She played the flute in her school band. One fall the band members sold candy to raise money for a band trip. Carol says, "I sold more candy than anyone else, even though I was really scared to talk to people I didn't know. When I told my dad that I had won the sales contest, he said, 'I know how you can sell even more. I'll take you down to the mall this Saturday.' In spite of all I'd done, he still expected me to do more."

One day when Carol came home from school, her mother was drunk. As soon as she saw Carol, she began to scream, "How dare you leave your room in such a mess? You fat, lazy slob! You're just a fat slob! Tell me, what did I ever do to have such a lazy, ugly kid?" Carol didn't say anything. She went to her room to clean up. As she dusted her dresser, she studied her reflection in the mirror. That night, Carol began her diet by cutting her servings in half. She made sure that she didn't eat everything on her plate. She started a jogging routine—two or three miles every morning, followed by an hour of heavy exercise.

By the time Carol entered the hospital a year-and-a-half later, her weight had dropped from 120 pounds to 78. She had reduced her daily calories to 600. She exercised all the time. She wiggled her toes or pressed her legs together while sitting. She did knee bends or ran in place while standing. Carol was afraid that if she wasn't burning calories all the time, she would gain weight.

Carol agreed to enter the hospital only after the whole family went through *counseling*. Counseling means talking to a trained expert to help solve problems. Her mother had begun treatment for alcoholism. Together the family tackled some of the problems they were having. After 12 weeks in the hospital, Carol got her weight up to 90 pounds. She began to question her view of herself as "fat." She continued to see a *therapist* (another word for counselor) to help her work out her emotional problems.

Today Carol is still underweight, but she has given up thinness as the most important goal in her life. "Now my goal is to get well," she says. "Food doesn't control me like it used to. I've worked hard to change that. Recovering has meant hashing out a lot of conflicts with my mom and dad. I'm not afraid of them anymore, though. I've learned to love myself a little. I've learned to ask others for help."

WHAT HAPPENS TO THE BULIMIC?

Bulimics are people who have put themselves in a trap. Terrified of getting fat, they diet constantly. They forbid themselves even a taste of their favorite foods. Yet food is a source of comfort to them. Most bulimics enjoy the taste and texture of food, even though they

Bulimics diet constantly and will not allow themselves even a taste of their favorite food.

fear what food will do to their bodies.

Many bulimics say that binging and purging gives them a sense of relief from their *anxieties*. During a binge, they think only about what they are eating, what they will eat next, and how to stuff the food in their mouths even faster. Binging becomes a form of escape. It is a way of taking their minds off other problems.

After the binge the bulimic will be very full—and

very afraid. She may have eaten more calories in an hour or so than most women eat all day. This makes her panic. She thinks she must immediately rid her body of all the unwanted calories.

To purge the calories, the bulimic may vomit, take a large dose of laxatives, exercise very hard, or all three. Most bulimics vomit. Some, after emptying their stomachs, may return to the binge. They may repeat the cycle several times before they finish. After a binge and purge cycle, many bulimics report a feeling of mental and emotional numbness.

Finally remorse and guilt begin to creep in. The bulimic feels she has "failed" again. Many bulimics vow, after each binge, that they will never binge again.

Food is a source of comfort to some bulimics even though they fear what food will do to their bodies.

They say they will never, ever eat a particular food again. Tomorrow, they promise themselves, they will be back on their diets again. From now on, they will be "in control." Unfortunately, setting these new, stricter standards often sets the bulimic up for her next failure.

Some bulimics feel that if they take even one bite of a "forbidden" food, they have ruined or failed their diets. "Oh well," they reason, "now I've blown it. I might as well go ahead and binge." The loss of control again produces feelings of guilt and shame. The bad feelings lead to another binge, another purge, more guilt, and so on.

SYMPTOMS OF BULIMIA

The symptoms of bulimia are not as obvious as those of anorexia. Anorexia is known by a weight loss, a fear of getting fat, and a refusal to gain weight. But bulimia is defined by the behavior itself. Some bulimics begin as anorectics. And most anorectics will sometimes binge and purge. Most bulimics, however, will be fairly close to their "natural" weight. Even though their weights may go up and down, bulimics give few outward signs of their disorder. Because their binges take place in secret, many bulimics suffer for years without anyone finding out.

Most bulimics will stay fairly close to their natural weight.

PHYSICAL AND EMOTIONAL PROBLEMS

Bulimia is harder to identify than anorexia, but the physical problems are just as harmful. Women who are bulimic may suffer from irregular menstrual periods. Dental cavities are a problem because bulimics eat foods with a lot of sugar. Bulimics who purge by vomiting can cause permanent damage to their tooth enamel because of the stomach acid that washes over their teeth.

Binging and purging can also cause chemical imbalances in the body. This makes the bulimic prone to irregular heartbeat, kidney damage, or muscle spasms. If the heart or kidneys are damaged badly enough that they stop working, the victim will die. Other damages caused by repeated vomiting include a "chipmunk" face (caused by swollen salivary glands), a hoarse voice, and a torn or bleeding esophagus (food tube). Abuse of laxatives and diuretics can cause skin rashes, pimples, constipation, and a bloated abdomen.

Bulimics may suffer from some or all of the physical problems. The emotional damage can be even more painful. Secrecy, shame, and a feeling of being totally alone are the emotional effects of bulimia. Cut off from family and friends by her secrecy, a bulimic thinks she is the only person in the whole world who has this problem.

ONE BULIMIC'S STORY

Sue is a 30-year-old woman who was bulimic for 14 years. She says she never even knew the name of her disorder until she had been that way for nine years. It took five years after she first heard the word "bulimia" for Sue to decide she wanted to get well.

Sue began her bulimia at age 16 with a very strict diet. She was in a group of four girls who were all sensitive about their weight. They all dieted. One night they all went on a binge together. Then one of

Some bulimics start their binging and purging habits because their friends do it.

The first goal in treating bulimia is to stop the cycle of binging and purging.

them had the idea to vomit the food back up so she wouldn't gain weight. Little did Sue realize the habit she began that night would take 14 years to break.

After high school, Sue went on to college, and then got married. Her new husband did not know about her bulimia. Sue was terrified about what would happen when he found out.

The pressure of keeping the secret seemed to make the bulimia worse. She would binge and purge when her husband wasn't home. Then she had to go out and buy more food so he wouldn't notice how much was gone. Sue made sure she didn't go to the same grocery store too often.

She was embarrassed about how much food she had to buy — and how often she had to buy it. Money started to be a problem. Sue had to take money out of her savings account so her husband wouldn't notice how much money she spent on food.

No one can keep a secret forever. Before long, Sue's husband learned of her bulimia. At first he tried to be understanding and encouraged her to get well. But Sue wasn't ready to get well. Bulimia had become part of her life. It was her way of coping with problems. Even though she hated herself and the way she was acting, Sue was afraid to stop. Sue's husband got frustrated with her. He felt she was refusing to take care of herself. His attitude turned to anger and disgust, and they finally divorced.

After the divorce, Sue began to feel desperate. She was short of money, lonely, and insecure. She knew she needed to get help, but where? She thought about putting herself in the hospital for treatment, but her medical insurance would not pay for it. She couldn't afford to pay for it herself. She began going to a counselor and joined a bulimia *support group.*

In the group, Sue learned how bulimia affects the body. She explored new ways to cope with problems. Her counselor kept assuring her that she was not hopeless. "There's a way through it," he said over and over. To help Sue learn to love herself, he suggested that she start a "daily affirmation" book. It was a diary where she could write something good about herself every day. "People like me because..." or "Today I accomplished..." are some examples of affirmations.

Sue worked with the group and her counselor. She began to feel good about herself for the first time in her life. She began to build self-esteem. She learned not to overload herself with goals that she would never be able to live up to. Above all, Sue learned to talk about her problems. Before she told her friends about her bulimia, Sue was afraid they would reject her. As she began to share her secret, she found that others still accepted her. By being honest with herself and others, she was able to stop feeling ashamed.

After 14 years of being bulimic and several years of therapy, Sue finally feels she has stopped the bulimia. How does she feel about the disease now that she has recovered? Sue says, "I hated being bulimic. It was very expensive. It wasted a lot of time. I isolated myself. I felt that no one could ever love me. I am extremely glad to be free of it!"

TREATMENT

Eating disorders are curable, but the sooner the treatment begins, the better the chances for success. There are no facts available on how many of the anorectics or bulimics who seek treatment actually

During therapy, many anorectics and bulimics learn to talk about their problems with other people.

recover fully. No one knows for sure how many of them will stay well over the course of time. The longer eating disorder victims go without treatment, the more likely it is that they will suffer permanent damage.

There are three goals in the treatment of eating disorders. The first is to stop the self-destructive behavior. This means coaxing the anorectic to eat and gain weight. It means helping the bulimic to stop binging. The second goal is to help the victim change her body image. Neither anorectics nor bulimics will give up their behavior for very long unless they realize they are not "fat." They must believe that they do not need to stick to such strict eating habits. The final goal is to prevent relapse. That means to help the victims avoid falling back into old behaviors.

Anorectics and bulimics must learn new ways of facing stress, as Carol did. They must build self-esteem, as Sue did. Above all, if anorectics and bulimics want to recover, they must accept the fact that they have a problem, but the problem is *not* their weight. It is their behavior.

STOPPING THE SELF-DESTRUCTIVE BEHAVIOR

Treatment that takes place inside a hospital is called *in-patient treatment*. This option is often chosen for anorectics. They are less likely to admit they have a problem (bulimics, on the other hand, know their behavior is abnormal, but they don't know how to stop). The patient's eating can be watched more closely in a hospital than at home. By restricting access to bathrooms, the hospital staff can prevent the patients from vomiting their food after meals.

The patients receive daily reports about their progress. Before being admitted to the hospital, the anorectic or bulimic will be examined and tested to make sure there is no physical cause, such as disease, for her condition.

An anorectic or bulimic is examined before she enters the hospital to make sure there are no physical reasons for her conditions.

Unless there is an emergency such as a physical collapse, the anorectic should not be forced into the hospital against her will. She and her family must agree that hospitalization is necessary. Otherwise, she will resist treatment and have less chance for success.

Before any other kind of therapy can begin, the anorectic must gain some weight. This is a challenge because gaining weight is the anorectic's greatest fear. Yet unless she can gain enough weight to regain her ability to think clearly, other forms of therapy will be wasted. One successful method is *behavioral therapy.* Behavioral therapy focuses on changing behavior by rewarding good behavior and punishing bad behavior.

During behavioral therapy, patients receive praise and privileges (such as visitors or TV rights) if they eat and gain weight. If they fail to eat or to gain weight, privileges are denied. This gives the patients a reason to want to gain weight.

The hospital serves large, well-balanced meals. Sometimes a patient may be too uncomfortable or too afraid to eat solid food. She may receive a nourishing malt-type drink. If she resists eating and drinking entirely, the anorectic may have to be fed *intravenously* (liquid nutrients are injected into a vein by means of a needle). The hospital staff records how much and what kinds of foods each patient takes in at each meal. Every day the patients are weighed. They learn from the staff how many calories they have taken in.

Gradually, if the treatment is successful, the anorectics will relearn more normal eating patterns. They will gain weight slowly. They will slowly overcome their fears. They will realize that eating a "forbidden" food will not make them instantly or uncontrollably fat.

INCREASING SELF-ESTEEM

Once the anorectic has gained weight, a therapist

A therapist can help the anorectic or bulimic gain self-esteem.

can begin to change her body image. Counseling therapy begins in the hospital and continues after the patient leaves. The therapist challenges the anorectic's self-image. He or she helps the patient understand her need for "control" and helps her let go of thinness as her main goal in life. By helping the patient develop new ways of coping, a trained therapist can prevent a relapse.

The first goal in treating bulimia is to stop the cycle of dieting, binge eating, and purging. If the bulimic feels too out of control, she may admit herself to the hospital. In most cases, though, bulimics can be treated on an *out-patient* basis.

Many therapists will urge the bulimic to talk to family and friends about her disorder. Talking helps reduce guilt, secrecy, and loneliness. The therapist encourages the patient to keep a journal to discover the feelings that lead to binging. Together, patient and counselor work to change the poor body image that led to the diet in the first place.

The bulimic also receives nutrition education. After years of "forbidden" foods, fear of getting fat, and binging and purging, many bulimics have lost all sense of what it means to eat a balanced diet. Like the anorectics, they learn that they can eat normally without getting abnormally fat.

As the bulimic ends her binge-and-purge behavior, her therapist will help her to build self-esteem, solve

Everyone needs someone else to talk to once in a while.

problems, face risks, deal with stress, and get help from her friends. Bulimics and anorectics may join eating disorder support groups. There they can discuss and work out their common problems.

WHAT TO DO

If someone has told you that you are fat, or if you feel you are "too fat," think for a moment. The person who said it could be wrong! Talk to your parents. Visit your family doctor or your school nurse. A qualified medical professional can tell you what's the normal weight for a person of your age and height.

If it is your parents who want you to lose (or gain) weight, they should be willing to take you to the doctor for nutritional and exercise counseling. If one of your friends is on an unusual diet, tell her to see a doctor or nurse about it, too.

If your friend has an eating disorder, she might refuse to get help. She might accuse you of being jealous or trying to ruin her diet. If this happens, you need to tell someone else about your concern. Talk to your parents, an understanding teacher, or a school counselor. They may have some ideas about how to help your friend.

The most important thing to do is *talk about your problems!* Very few people—children or adults—can solve all their problems by themselves. By sharing our worries, fears, and insecurities, we learn ways to face them and overcome them.

FOR MORE INFORMATION

For more information on anorexia nervosa and bulimia, write to:

The Center for the Study of Anorexia and Bulimia
1 West 91st Street
New York, NY 10024

American Anorexia/Bulimia Association
133 Cedar Lane
Teaneck, NJ 07666

National Association of Anorexia Nervosa
and Associated Disorders
P.O. Box 271
Highland Park, IL 60035

GLOSSARY/INDEX

ADOLESCENCE 19— *"Becoming adult." It begins with the onset of puberty (usually about age 10 or 12) and ends with the body's growth (usually about age 18 or 20).*

BEHAVIORAL THERAPY 39, 40— *A method of changing behavior by rewarding good and punishing bad behavior.*

BINGE 6, 21, 27, 28, 29, 32, 33, 34, 43— *To eat an unusually large amount of food in a short time.*

CALORIE 11, 40— *A unit for measuring the amount of energy our bodies get from food. Different kinds of food have higher or lower amounts of calories.*

COUNSELING 25, 35, 36, 40, 44— *Meeting with a specially-trained person who listens to you, talks to you, and helps you sort out your problems.*

CRASH DIET 16, 22— *A diet that promises very rapid weight loss. Crash diets usually involve eating limited kinds of foods, so they are not safe. After losing weight on a crash diet, most people gain the weight right back.*

DEPRESSION 21— *A state of feeling very sad for a long time. Depression can make it hard for a person to think, make decisions, and get along with others.*

DIURETICS 7— *Drugs that cause the body to shed water by increasing the urine flow. Overuse of diuretics can make a person quite sick.*

GLOSSARY/INDEX

FASTING 7 — *A time when a person does not eat, or eats very little. Some people fast for religious purposes, but this is only for a short time. Fasting is not a healthy way to lose weight.*

INTRAVENOUS FEEDING 40 — *Provides nutrients in a liquid form through a tube and needle directly into a vein.*

LANUGO 23 — *A fine covering of hair that grows on the body.*

LAXATIVES 5, 6, 11, 28, 32 — *Drugs that cause you to have a bowel movement. Overuse of laxatives can make it very hard for a person to have a bowel movement when he stops taking the drugs.*

NUTRITION 43 — *Providing proteins, minerals, vitamins, calories and other elements necessary for body function. With good nutrition, you stay healthy. With bad nutrition, you get sick.*

PUBERTY 17, 19 — *The age at which a boy or girl is first able to reproduce. The beginning of sexual maturity.*

PURGE 6, 27, 28, 29, 32, 34, 43 — *To get rid of something unwanted. Anorectics and bulimics are afraid of food, so they want to empty their bodies of all food.*

SELF-ESTEEM 17, 21, 36, 43 — *How you feel about*

yourself. If you like yourself, you have high self-esteem. If you feel bad about yourself, you have low self-esteem.

SET-POINT 12 — *The body's "natural" weight. If you are not ill, are eating a healthy diet, and getting a moderate amount of exercise, your body will tend to stay at its natural weight.*

SUPPORT GROUP 35, 44 — *A group of people who have a similar problem. They meet regularly to talk about their problems and encourage each other.*

THERAPIST OR COUNSELOR 26, 40, 43 — *A specially-trained person who listens to you, talks to you about your problems, and helps you sort them out.*

TREATMENT, IN-PATIENT AND OUT-PATIENT 36, 37, 38, 39, 43 — *For in-patient treatment, a person enters the hospital and stays there while being treated. For out-patient treatment, the person does not stay at the hospital, but comes there for the treatment sessions.*